Podcasting Success in a Day
By Sam Key

Beginner's Guide to Fast, Easy, and Efficient Learning of Podcasting
2nd Edition

Table of Contents

Introduction 3

Chapter 1 – Podcasting 101: The Basics 4

Chapter 2 – Getting Started with Podcasting: The Equipment to be used 9

Chapter 3 – Step-by-Step Guide to Podcasting Success 13

Chapter 4 – Techniques in Getting People to Subscribe to your Podcast 21

Chapter 5 – The Pre-Podcast Checklist: Things to Do Before Recording your Podcast 24

Chapter 6 – Podcast Interviews: What to Do and How to Do It 30

Chapter 7 – Sharing your Podcast: Where to Post Them and How 37

Chapter 8 – Going Live: Take your Podcast to Another Level 43

Conclusion 50

Check out my other Books 51

Introduction

I want to thank you and congratulate you for purchasing the book, *"Podcasting Success in a Day! – Beginner's Guide to Fast, Easy and Efficient Learning of Podcasting"*.

This book contains proven steps and strategies on how to become successful in the world of podcasting and release your first podcast as soon as possible with our easy-to-follow guidelines.

Not knowing what and how to do something even if you are interested in it can be difficult. Sometimes, your interest in it may not be enough to guarantee success. With the help of this book, we will provide you with the basic information that you need regarding podcasting. We will also guide you on how you can make your first podcast and provide effective techniques on how to increase your subscribers and listeners.

Thanks again for purchasing this book, I hope you enjoy it!

Chapter 1 – Podcasting 101: The Basics

While it's true that technology has given people with more options for communicating, it doesn't necessarily imply that traditional methods of conveying a message are not effective. In fact, the new communication methods being used today are simply small improvements over the traditional ones. One such method, which combined the Internet and audio or video recording, is the podcast.

This chapter will discuss what podcasting is and answer some of the questions that will help you to better understand it.

What's a podcast?

A podcast is an audio or video recording uploaded over the Internet. Podcasts are very similar to radio programs as each podcast talks about a certain topic or explores a particular issue. There are times that the podcast invites guests or experts that can discuss the topic better than them, just like what's done in radio programs.

Podcasts can be further divided into different episodes, where each episode is a part of the whole issue or topic being discussed. Think of podcast episodes as a discussion of specific concepts found on the general topic. In most cases, podcast owners release several episodes as part of one topic.

What makes a podcast different from an audio file?

While these two share the same qualities, one distinguishable difference between them is that podcasts are compiled in an RSS feed for easier access while audio files are not. If you are subscribed to an RSS feed of a podcast, new episodes are readily downloaded and provided to you by the program. This is unlike audio files where you have to manually look for the latest episode and download it.

Another possible and probably most obvious difference is that podcasts are audio files uploaded over the Internet and can be accessed or downloaded in an RSS and can be subscribed to. On the other hand, audio files are simply recorded messages that may or may not be uploaded or downloaded, and cannot be subscribed to.

Do I need special equipment in order to access podcasts?

Podcasts are readily accessible by listeners. They can access podcasts through online streaming or by purchasing the file through RSS or web syndication. Downloaded files, in turn, can be uploaded on any media player, which makes it possible for people to listen to the content whenever they want or wherever they are.

While the term podcast features the word "pod', which features the contribution of iPod's popularity in its popularity, podcasts can be listened to using any media player, whether portable or not.

Why should you consider podcasting?

While the more prominent presentation methods such as blogs or infographics don't look like they're going to fade into obsolescence anytime soon, podcasting is one of the rising avenues of presenting content to people. According to a research done in the US, there has been a steady increase on the consumption of podcasts in the last few years. From an estimate of 9% in 2008, the percentage of podcast listeners has increased to 15% in 2014. This increasing trend on the number of listeners simply implies that it is one of the avenues worth considering by businesses or digital marketers in the future.

The following are other good reasons that will explain why podcasting is a good avenue market your business or expertise:

- Podcasting can increase your website traffic – The increasing trend of podcast listeners only implies that people are interested in this medium. Unfortunately, few websites are utilizing podcasts as of today. In order for your website to experience a significant boost in its average visitors, you have to offer them something that cannot be easily found on other websites. By being one of the few sites that provide podcasts, there is a huge possibility that listeners will subscribe and follow your content.

- For businesses, it can be used as a marketing tool and can increase conversions – If your website is selling something, podcasts can be used both to introduce your products and to increase the possibility that casual visitors can be turned into subscribers and, eventually, buyers. Podcasts can be offered as freebies when visitors do subscribe to your email list or RSS feed. As a marketing tool, you can use a few minutes of your podcast to endorse what you're selling or recommend something that is included in your store's inventory. When the information that you provide is found to be useful by listeners, they might be enticed to buy the product. The "human touch" provided by the use of voice can be more enticing compared to written content.

- Customer or visitor engagement is improved with podcasts – As mentioned, a podcast can be considered as a good marketing tool because of its human touch. This same element can also be used so that subscribers will be more engaged. Voice conveys more meaning or emotion compared to written words. Podcasts can even be used as a way to reach out to listeners, as you can ask how they find your episode or if there are other topics that they want you to discuss or cover. Since podcasts sound like you're directly talking to the listener, they are more likely to provide comments and increase engagement to your website. Increased engagement, in turn, is one way to give your site a boost on its SERP ranking. Because search engines will deem your site helpful due to the comments found in it, the chances of people noticing your website are further increased.

- Podcasts can help improve your (or the website's) image – Releasing podcasts about a certain topic gives the impression that you are an expert in the area or field being discussed. While this can be achieved through written content, talking about it only implies that your ideas are correct and/or should be believed by listeners. This will help visitors identify you as better than others who tackle the same topics as you do. This, in turn, will result in increased credibility in your area of expertise and eventually lead to more people visiting your site.

Now that podcasting and the benefits that can be gained with its use have been discussed, it will be easier to see why it is a medium that should be utilized in delivering content over the Internet.

Chapter 2 – Getting Started with Podcasting: The Equipment to be used

Podcasting requires recording of the voice while the person discusses something. But as somebody new to this medium, you might ask about the equipment needed to start with podcasting. After all, you cannot hope to get the benefits of releasing a podcast if the equipment used to capture the voice and discussion is inappropriate.

This chapter will enumerate what aspiring podcasters will need in order to record their content.

Recording device

The most obvious piece of equipment that podcasters MUST have is a recording device. In order to produce an audio file, you need equipment that has the ability to record your voice.

A recording device can take many forms – all thanks to the continuous improvement of technology. Here are some of the devices that will help record your discussion:

- The simplest recording device is the Dictaphone. Similar to the cassette tape recorder, it is mostly used by scientists or medical experts to record procedures. It records audio files that can be uploaded on a computer and be reviewed by transcriptionists that will then transcribe the recording into written form.

- Laptops have built-in microphones that can be used to record your discussions. This will save you some money as there is no need to buy a separate recording device.

The audio file can also be edited as soon as the recording is finished, as it is saved on your laptop.

- Mobile phones, whether old models or smart phones, may have a recorder. Since mobile phones are primarily used for calling, you can be assured that it can record your voice clearly.

Which recording device should you utilize?

Since all of the devices mentioned above can record voice, all that's left for you to consider would be your budget and certain situations. If you have money, then you can consider buying high-end portable recording devices. These devices often have features that may not be found in their lower-priced alternatives. Situations that you might consider involve the number of people that you will be asking to guest on your episode, the need to travel, or the location of the recording. For example, the laptop may be doing two tasks at the same time, but you may want to consider getting a Dictaphone if you see yourself recording in other places very often. Dictaphones also eliminate the need for setting up any equipment as recordings can be done instantaneously.

Microphone

Another device that might be useful for recording your discussion is the microphone. This has the purpose of amplifying the sounds picked up by the recording device. This is helpful if you or the guest in your show speaks in a low voice or volume as this makes the words come out clear on the recording device and on your podcast.

Some guidelines in choosing a microphone

While it is not entirely important to purchase a microphone to make your podcast, doing so will greatly enhance the quality of your product. However, if you are using a laptop or PC to record, it is highly necessary that you use a microphone. This is because the built-in microphones on these devices do not always ensure a recording of good quality.

If you are to buy a microphone, make sure that it is compatible with your recording device. Many Dictaphones and mobile phones have jacks where the microphone can be attached, making it easier to record high-quality audio files even if multiple guests for your show are asked to speak.

Podcast editing software

The need for software to edit your podcast depends on your accuracy; if you (or your guest) can discuss or say everything without mistakes or stutters, then it is possible to do a podcast without it. Oftentimes, however, you will be making mistakes while speaking. There is also the possibility that your recording device captures too many unnecessary sounds, and these can significantly lower the quality of your podcast. If these happen, then it is important that you have a program that will help you to stitch different parts of your recording or remove the unwanted.

Call recording program

It is not always possible to get other people to come to your recording location and talk about a topic. However, it is still possible to get statements from experts with a little help from technology. Using the call recording software, it is possible to contact experts via Skype or similar programs and record what they could share to your listeners. While this is not necessary to have, it can help bridge the distance and still record what the experts have to say.

If you are one of those who do not want to start podcasting because you don't know which equipment you should have, then all you need are the materials mentioned above. Once you do, you now have the ability to produce your own podcast.

Chapter 3 – Step-by-Step Guide to Podcasting Success

Now that you already know the equipment needed to record your discussion, it's time to take action and start making your own podcast.

This chapter will run through the steps that should be taken in order to start making podcasts. Guidelines on how to provide good quality podcasts will also be enumerated.

Start with the basics of your podcast

"Even the most successful podcaster started at the bottom."

This should be your mindset when you have decided to make podcasts. It is helpful to look at established podcasters and emulate the actions that made them established. However, it wouldn't help if you compare your achievements to theirs. Remember that they became successful by tracking on their own progress and not that of others.

In starting your podcast, it is important that you have thought about the following:

- Podcast name – Think of it as a company name, something which will be used by listeners to identify you. Make sure that the podcast name is catchy and gives listeners an idea as to what your podcast is about.

- What you're planning to talk about – Next to the name would be the content that you'll provide to listeners. Make sure that every podcast episode talks about the topic that you know will be helpful to your audience.

- Artwork – Along with the description text, giving aesthetic appeal to your listeners could somehow influence whether they'll subscribe to your podcasts or not.

Specify how often you will be releasing your podcast

Having a schedule for posting is also important in podcasting. People are more likely to subscribe to your podcast if you provide new content on a regular basis. No matter what schedule you decide to follow (whether every day, once a week, or once a month), consistency should be the key.

Identifying the schedule for posting, though, depends on you (a day when you have time to work on your podcast) or the audience (which day of the week or month do you have the most visitors).

To prevent yourself from not being able to follow your schedule, make sure that you have a podcast "stock". Not only will this give you enough time to research, record, and edit, it will also enable you to provide teasers so that listeners will eagerly await the next episodes.

Make sure that you'll present great content

Even if you do know the general topic that you'll be covering in your podcast, it is necessary to choose specific topics that should be discussed in detail and to present them in the best possible manner.

When it comes to presentation, make sure that the delivery of the content is enjoyable and beneficial to the listeners. See to it that the material that you will discuss cannot be found anywhere else. The structure of your presentation should be in a way that will allow for easier comprehension (presenting the basics before delving into more complicated areas).

Lastly, consider improving the quality of your speaking voice. This will serve as the "icing" of your great content, as the material will be delivered clearly.

Will you prepare a script or not?

One possible question that can be asked by those who are new to podcasting would be if they will be writing a script for their episode or not. Even those who are experienced in podcasting cannot give a definite answer to this question.

While it is true that the answer to this question depends on who will be making the podcast, there are certain benefits and drawbacks of recording with or without a script.

For those who will use a script, the main advantage would be that they will be able to cover every area related to the episode's topic. The script will also guide them as to what to say next, making it possible to record without having to edit and remove long pauses or stutters. It is also easier for you to release the transcription of your podcast. However, its main drawback would be that the effort needed to produce one content is doubled; aside from writing what you need to deliver, there also is the effort to record it. There is also the possibility that the delivery of the material will be "robotic"; not being able to back-up the material with an accompanying emotion somehow makes the speaker unfriendly and un-spontaneous.

On the other hand, not using a full script (just an outline) could save you time as well as make the delivery of the material more natural. This non-robotic way of recording could make you sound more engaging and personal. What makes this method disadvantageous, though, is that it is almost impossible to say what you want or need to say if you only have a rough outline; this is true even if you're an expert on the topic being discussed. There is also the possibility of stuttering or finding yourself lost for words. These can be captured on your recording, which makes editing inevitable (as well as time-consuming).

Identify how long your podcast will be

Another important aspect that could determine whether or not your podcast will become popular to people would be the length of your podcast.

The average amount of time that an adult can stay attentive at a lecture is around 15 to 20 minutes. This simply implies that if your podcast goes way past this average, it is highly likely that listeners will be discouraged from subscribing to your podcast.

However, this doesn't mean that you should always strive to make your podcasts short. There are podcasts which further exceed the average amount of time but still experience success. The decision as to the length of your podcast still depends on you. As long as the information and explanation that you can provide to listeners is sufficient, then the length should not be a problem. One possible solution that can be applied in order to trim your podcast length to the average would be to simplify the points that you (or your show's guest) will be providing to the listeners. By doing so, you can be sure that listeners will stay attentive to the content provided on your podcasts while providing them enough information about the topic being discussed.

Ask experts to be a guest on your podcast

The presence of somebody else, most especially an expert on the topic being discussed, has been mentioned in the previous sections. But why would you need to invite a guest speaker when you can research and talk about the topic yourself?

This is because of the following reasons:

- Having a guest speaker can greatly boost the quality of the material being discussed – If somebody who knows the field will be presenting the topic, you will be getting more inputs compared to when an unknowledgeable person researches about it. The guest can further elaborate the basics that you have researched, explain it in a manner that can be easily comprehended by listeners, and even provide unique information that only individuals with enough experience will know.

- It improves the credibility of your podcast – When you get an expert to speak on your podcast, it creates the impression that your show is providing credible and accurate information. This, in turn, will result in listeners deeming your podcast as one that can provide them with what they need when it comes to the field or topic that you're discussing.

- Experts can give your podcast a slight improvement in its number of listeners – If the expert that you're interviewing is quite popular, there is a huge possibility that their audience will subscribe to your podcast and hear what the expert has to say.

In most cases though, it can be very difficult to get experts to guest in a podcast – whether you'll be talking with them over the phone or inviting them to your recording studio. However, it is possible for them to share some of their time if what you're asking them to discuss are simple areas that fall under your topic. To make this possible, you need to submit an invitation stating why you chose them as a resource speaker and what you want them to share on your podcast. Don't forget to ask them if they can guest on your podcast or not.

▯ecord at the right place while using the right e▯uip▯ ent

In the previous chapter, we enumerated the equipment necessary for recording your podcast. But aside from the equipment, the place where your recording will take place is also important.

It is not necessarily important to record your podcast in a studio. However, it is necessary that you set up your recording in a place that is absolutely quiet or at least free from auditory distractions (This involves even the subtlest background noise.). Small as they may be, these sounds can ruin the overall quality of the podcast and even mess up the message that you want to share to your listeners.

Some of the factors that you could look at when choosing the place where you do your recording are the following:

- Your recording location should be far from sources of noise such as corridors or windows that are facing the street.

- Make sure that equipment such as computers are not running in the background. Otherwise, they should at least be at a reasonable distance away from the microphone or recording device.

- To prevent echoes, conduct the recording in a large room. Also avoid recording near the walls.

- If you have guests coming over, make sure that anything which can cause noise is removed prior to recording (Sometimes, they're the biggest cause of unnecessary sounds.). Some of the noises that you can prepare for are jangling keys, coughing or sniffing, and moving the recorder.

?earn the art of asking ?uestions

If you are doing the podcast with a guest, the questions that you'll be asking them could make or break your show. Make sure that you only ask great questions to your guests.

Great questions are identified as such if they are structured in a way that will provide the most useful information to your listeners. If the question you need to ask seems to be weak, restructure it so that you get the answer that you want.

Another good practice when asking questions is to do so after the expert delivers his/her answer. Only interrupt the person if it is absolutely necessary (such as if the answer is far from what you're asking them or if the guest mentions expletive words). Letting them finish before asking another question could result in weak conversations (i.e. The guest will not want to speak anymore.), poor audio quality, and even a ticked off guest.

?repare for editing

Now that you've done the recording, the editing follows. This is where you remove the unnecessary parts during the recording process so that the podcast will be flawless. This is also where you can stitch additional parts so as to improve the product.

How about additional music or sound effects?

One question that needs to be answered by those new to podcasting is if they will be adding sound effects over the course of their podcast. This is because sound effects can make podcasts interesting and stand out over other similar podcasts. Even a short musical intro and repeated sound effects (such as clapping or "crowd sounds") can make your show distinguishable by listeners. It can also serve as fillers for silent moments, such as when you are waiting for a response from the guest or when you're taking a break before starting to speak again.

One potential problem that is faced by those who would want to use sound effects, though, is finding a source for the sound that they want. Although it is possible for them to do it in their own, it may not be as good as those heard on radio programs or other popular podcasts. Fortunately, the Internet can point you to different sites that offer royalty-free music and sound effects. Simply acknowledge the creator or source in your show, and you can use the audio file as often as you like without having to shell out money.

After editing, your podcast is now ready for posting. By following the steps and guidelines mentioned above, recording your succeeding podcasts will become a breeze.

Chapter 4 – Techniques in Getting People to Subscribe to your Podcast

Simply recording your podcast doesn't necessarily imply that people interested to podcasts will automatically swarm to your website and listen to your podcast. You also need to promote your podcast and get people to subscribe in order to increase the number of your listeners.

This chapter will enumerate the techniques that can be utilized in order to promote your podcast as well as gain more listeners.

Create a great headline for your podcast

Just like written content, headlines are necessary if you want your podcast to be noticed by others. If your headline is well-written, people will be more compelled to continue listening to your podcast. This is also one way to get indexed by search engines; the words you use on your headline could help them in suggesting your feed to individuals who type similar terms in their search box.

One technique that you should utilize when writing your headline is to make sure that you provide the main message that you would want to convey to your listeners. You can also include the benefits that they can gain by listening to your podcast. This will somehow stir the curiosity of the listener, which in turn influences them into subscribing and listening to the podcast. Make sure to mention pain points or important issues so that people searching over the Internet can easily find your podcast.

?tili?e podcast directories

Just like what bloggers do in order to increase their readership, podcast owners can also submit their podcast feed to directories so that they can be easily found and promoted. This is also one way to get to know other podcasters and learn from them.

Asking guests to share the podcast

It may be too much to ask of your guest to promote your podcast, but it is one of the most direct ways to get additional listeners for the said podcast. Fortunately, experts will comply to this request simply because they are also promoting themselves. Ask them to share the podcast either through social media sites or mention your link to those subscribed to their email list.

Integrate plugins on your website for easier subscription

While it is true that sharing is necessary for the podcast to have more listeners, you still need to make it easier for people to subscribe and share your content. Fortunately, it is possible for you to install plugins which makes the task of subscribing to your feed and sharing your content to social media sites possible with just a few clicks.

?onsider offering bonuses when a person subscribes

Unfortunately, it is possible for listeners to simply download your podcast and refuse interaction or have a connection to you – that is, not subscribing to your podcast feed. If you want to become known in the field of your choice, you will need more subscribers. So, what can you do to get them engaged? Offer them something that they cannot get unless they're subscribed!

Some of the bonuses that you can give subscribers include "exclusive" content that are not included on the released podcast and may be more helpful to them. You can also consider giving them a transcribed copy of the episode so that it will be easier for them to follow and remember what was discussed in your podcast. This is also an opportunity for you to cover another medium even with one content!

By applying the techniques mentioned above, getting listeners and subscribers for your podcast will be an easier task.

Chapter 5 – The Pre-Podcast Checklist: Things to Do Before Recording your Podcast

Preparation is a key element in creating a great podcast. Once you've got all your equipment ready, don't just hit record. In order to save valuable time fixing the recording during post-production, it's a great idea to plan ahead. A podcast takes a lot of time to produce, but spending some of it doing a little bit of preparation can go a long way in reducing time spent editing the audio file during post production.

This chapter contains a checklist of things to do before recording a podcast, as well as some tips for making a show outline and other things that can make the entire process of recording run as smooth as it possibly can.

The Pre-Production Checklist

Editing can resolve most of the issues that arise while recording a podcast; however, this process can be time-consuming and a little bit frustrating, especially if you're not getting the results you want. This is where pre-production comes in. The pre-production process involves creating a master plan to be followed to avoid running into problems during the recording and post-production of the podcast. This checklist will help you make the necessary preparations for your podcast recording.

- Create a show outline – Show outlines don't just list down the points you would want to discuss with your listeners. They also include technical details such as what music (if any) to use and when to insert them into the recording, as well as the special sound effects to be used in certain sections of the podcast. Aside from making sure that you cover all the topics and subtopics you need to cover, you can also use the show outline as the basis for a script if you decide to make one.

- Organize your materials – One of the issues that commonly arise when recording a podcast is not being able to find the audio clip or reference material that you need when you need it. Make sure you have all the audio files you need in one folder for easier access. If you're referencing a passage from any published material, it's always a good idea to have a hard copy of the material with the excerpt to be referenced highlighted. This way, you can avoid instances of dead air while looking for the passage you need.

- Do a test recording – Many people often find themselves having to re-do an entire recording because of issues with volume, white noise, and other audio problems. Most of these problems can be fixed during editing, but it would make things so much easier if you can nip it in the bud. A test recording will help you adjust the volume of the microphone, as well as the music clips and audio effects. This way, you'll have a balanced-sounding recording. It will also let you hear how you sound in the recording and you can adjust or modulate your voice accordingly.

Tips for Creating a Show outline

Recording on the fly is fine. A lot of people do it; however, you won't want to do that on your first try or until you get the hang of things. The show outline shows you exactly how your podcast will flow from what to play for your intro music to how you're going to end your podcast. A show outline can be as rough or as detailed as you want and in whatever format you wish to use (i.e. bullet points, table, etc...). As long as it keeps you on track, it's fine. Here are some tips in creating a good show outline:

Consider the flow of your podcast

The show outline is sort of the skeleton of the podcast. It should make it easy for you to connect one topic to the next. When creating a show outline, the overall flow of the show needs to be at the top of your list of considerations. Make sure you hit all the key points of your topic and arrange them in proper order. If needed, add sub-topics to the key points to make sure you got everything covered.

You should also divide your time wisely. There's really no rule on how the time should be used up, but you need to make sure that you allot enough time for each of your topics. Allot more time for points that are more difficult to explain and adjust the rest of your time accordingly. This way, you won't have to rush through discussing certain parts of your podcast or edit out chunks of it just to stay within your desired timeframe.

Make your outline easy to read

A show outline is used to keep the speaker from going off track while recording the podcast. If the outline is too complicated or is not written legibly enough, then it defeats the purpose of creating one. Keep it simple and clear so that it would be easy to read while recording. The show outline is not a script; it is just a guide. You don't need to write down everything you want to say in the outline itself. Having too many things on the show outline can be confusing to a lot of people, especially if you're not doing the podcast alone.

A good way to create a good outline is to type it out in a word processing program (MSWord, etc...) and print it out. Use simple and clear fonts and adjust the size so that it can be read clearly. Handwritten show outlines are okay; just make sure that the writing is legible and big enough to see. It is also a good idea to highlight important parts so that you don't accidentally skip them over while you are recording.

Include audio clips to be used in your outline

If you're planning to use sound effects, background music, and other musical or non-musical audio clips during your podcast, it's always advisable to include them in your show outline. This can help you get ready to play, pause or switch the audio files up when needed. When inserting the audio clips in your show outline, it's a good idea to highlight it or use a different font color to make them easier to identify.

If you're planning to use a lot of audio clips in your podcast, make sure to include the title or filename of the clip in your show outline so that you won't get confused and play the wrong one.

odcast criptwriting

A script can be very useful, especially for beginners. You won't have to worry about common issues like stuttering or skipping over key topics because everything you need to say is written there word for word. All you need to do is read it. Of course, using a script is optional, but if you do decide to create one for your show, the following tips can help you out:

Keep it conversational

People have the tendency to write down words that sound formal and even archaic at times. When writing a script, do it as if you were talking to a friend. Stay away from words that sound like it didn't come from this century or are hard to pronounce. Keep your sentences short so that your listeners won't get lost.

Also, avoid using words that are too technical if you can. Simplify it so that it would be easy to understand. Another advantage of using conversational language in your script is that it helps make it sound more natural when you say it out loud.

One more tip when writing your podcast script is to use words that stimulate a visual response from your listeners. Using words like "ballooned" rather than "increased" helps the listener visualize your words, making it more interesting to listen to and easier to understand and absorb.

Listen to your words

Your content may look good on paper, but it may not sound right when spoken. Practice reading the text out loud and listen to how you sound. If you sound stiff and robotic, you can easily make the necessary adjustment on the script or how you read it. Practice reading your script over and over until you can deliver it the best way you can.

If you find it hard to listen to your own voice while you are reading your script, do a test recording. It's easier to spot the things you need to change in your script or in your delivery when you hear yourself during playback.

Make your script readable

Just like with the show outline, you must be able to read your script clearly while recording. This will help you maintain a fluid, natural pace when reading your script. Use a simple font in a size that you can easily read.

Also, avoid writing long paragraphs to avoid losing your place in the script if you need to take your eyes away from it for a second.

Get a second opinion when you can

Having a second pair of eyes and ears can help you improve your script tremendously. Having someone read your script and critique it allows you to adjust mistakes that you didn't notice. He or she can also give you suggestions on how to improve your script even more.

It would be even better if you get him or her to listen as you read the script aloud. They can tell you if you're speaking too fast or too slow or if you sound like a robot while reading the script.

Once you've ticked all the boxes on your checklist and you have a proper show outline (or script), then it's time to start recording your podcast.

Chapter 6 – Podcast Interviews: What to Do and How to Do It

Having a guest speaker or interviewing a subject matter expert adds a lot of value to your podcast. Not only are you able to present another person's insights on the topic you are discussing; you can also expand your audience base in the process. Most guests – especially the high profile ones – bring in more than their expertise on the subject you wish to talk about; they bring in their fans as well. If you play your cards right, these people can subscribe to your podcast and become regular listeners.

In general, this chapter is all about dealing with guests on your podcast. To be specific, it will tackle where to find guests to invite and how to conduct interviews. It will also give you tips on the proper way to interview a guest speaker.

Inviting Guests to your Podcast

It's every podcaster's dream to be able to interview a high profile personality on their podcast, but that dream doesn't always come true. It's okay, though, because it doesn't matter if your guest is famous or not. What's important is that you have a guest who knows what he or she is talking about and is willing to share what they know to your listeners.

There are many ways to find people to interview. It can be as simple as asking a favor from a friend or as daunting as extending an invitation and booking a celebrity or high profile personality for your show and praying that they accept. Here are some strategies you can use to hook and book a guest on your podcast.

Contact people in your circle

As beginners, the first few interviews are the hardest to book. In this case, the easiest people to invite are the people in your network. They can be friends, relatives, or acquaintances who understand your topic well enough to answer your questions confidently and share valuable information with your listeners.

If none of the people within your circle fit the bill, you can ask them for referrals. One of them most likely knows someone who will be willing to speak to your listeners and answer your questions.

Utilize your social media connections

Most of the people you would want to interview have at least one social media account. If they actively share their knowledge and expertise using these accounts, then there's a good chance they would be willing to be interviewed to further widen their reach. Send them a short private message or a tweet to invite them to be your guests on your next podcast episode and wait for them to respond.

Don't be intimidated by the stature of the person you're inviting. The worst thing that could happen is that they would decline your invitation. Once you get a positive response, you can share contact info with each other and schedule the interview.

Scan podcast directories for similar podcasts

Some of the best interviewees have become guests in a lot of other podcasts. Check out other podcasts in your niche or in niches that are close to yours and see who their guests are. Listen to their interviews and choose someone who would be a good fit for your podcast. The next step is to search for their contact information and extend an invitation. If they've appeared as guests on more than two podcasts on the list, there's a greater chance that they will accept your invitation.

Ask your listeners who they would want to hear on your podcast

Taking requests from your audience may seem like an unorthodox way to find a guest for your podcast, but if you're running out of options, this is a great way to get suggestions. This way of finding a prospective guest has a lot of advantages to it. Aside from giving you names of people who they want to hear on your show, you can also ask them to post the questions they want to ask the guest as a way of making the show more interactive.

Find someone who has something to promote or sell

People who have products, books, videos, or their own podcasts to promote often jump at the chance to reach an audience. They need the exposure and you need a guest – it's a win-win situation. These people normally have their contact information on their websites, making it easy for you to send them a message.

Ask your guests for referrals

The best resource for guest speakers and interviewees are your guests themselves, especially if they've appeared as guests on other podcasts previously. This is a great way to expand your network and find more people who are qualified and are willing to be a guest on your podcast.

When inviting people to become guests on your podcast, make sure that you have all the information about your show written down. This includes the title of your show, the niche you cater to, your listener demographics and statistics, and the names of other people that you have interviewed on your podcast. Once you've sent your invitation, wait for them to respond. You can send follow-up emails if they take long to reply, but don't be pushy.

Don't worry if they decline or if they don't respond at all. You won't be able to book them all. Just move on to the next guest until you are able to book someone. Who knows? They may even be better interviewees than the high-profile personality you were after.

Conducting the Interview

Once you have a guest for your podcast, the next step is to figure out how to contact the guest for the actual interview. There are many ways to conduct an interview with someone who is not in the same room with you. Here are just some examples of ways to contact your interviewees:

- Over the phone – The simplest way to contact your interviewee is to call them on the phone and putting the call on speaker. This may be the easiest, but there are a lot of drawbacks to this method in terms of sound quality.

- 3rd Party Call-In Services – If you have money to spare, using a 3rd party service to contact your guests and record your interviews is the way to go. It works just like an online conference call service where the parties involved call in and enter a pin code to join the conversation. The call quality is generally good, especially if you have a fast internet connection and a lot of bandwidth to go with it. This method can also allow you to interview more than one guest at a time.

- Skype – This is the most convenient method to contact guests and conduct interviews. You can arrange for a Skype-to-Skype call or call the guest on their phones using the call-out service. Recording the conversation is a little trickier. Since Skype doesn't have a recording feature, you have to download a 3rd party application, which will allow you to record the conversation.

Inter⬚iew ⬚ti⬚uette⬚⬚ow to ⬚onduct a ⬚roper Inter⬚iew

Interviewing a guest is more than just the question and answer portion of your podcast. You need to be mindful of how you treat the interviewee from the moment you invite him or her to be a guest on your podcast to saying goodbye after the interview. The way you treat your interviewees will have an effect on the success of your show. If you don't treat your guests right, they may hesitate to speak during the interview, or worse, they may not show up at all.

Here are a few tips on how to conduct a proper interview.

- Be respectful of the guest's time. You are asking a potential guest to share some of his or her valuable time with you, so you should adjust to his or her schedule and not the other way around. Give the guest choices on the date and time the interview will take place and let them know how long the interview will run for. If your guest lives in a different time zone, always refer to the time in his or her time zone to prevent confusion. Also, send a follow-up email reminder the day before the scheduled interview.

- Be clear with the instructions you send. Many podcast interviews happen over the phone or VoIP applications. When you send the instructions to your guest, make sure that you include all the information he or she needs such as which platform will be used for the interview and who will make the call. There are some platforms that don't allow call-outs and the guests would have to call in for the interview. If this is the case, make sure you give the guest the correct phone number or ID to avoid having problems connecting.

- Send the guest a list of possible questions to be asked in the interview in advance. This will give them time to prepare their answers and let you know if there are topics that are off-limits. This will help you avoid talking about sensitive topics that may be offensive to the guest.

- In the event that you need to delay, postpone, or cancel the interview, inform the guest right away. Don't put this off until the last minute because they may think that you are wasting their precious time. Also, the earlier you let them know about the schedule change, the easier it will be to re-schedule the interview.

- As a courtesy and to remind the guest that the interview is about to begin, send him or her a message five minutes before the scheduled interview to check if he or she is ready. Whether you get a response or not, make sure you call the guest on time.

- Introduce the guest to your listeners. Do some research and say a few words about the person you are about to interview. Make sure that you pronounce his or her name correctly. If you're not sure about how to say their name, don't hesitate to ask them before the interview begins.

- Do not interrupt the guest during the interview unless it is absolutely necessary like when they use profane language or if they veer too far off topic.

- Show the guest that you're listening by giving verbal cues, just don't overdo it because it will sound like you are just agreeing with everything that they say without really listening.

- Ask open-ended questions and be prepared to ask follow-up questions when necessary.

- Avoid asking vague questions as this can lead the guest to veer off topic. If your guest starts straying from the topic being discussed, try not to interrupt unless absolutely necessary.

- Stick to your schedule. If going over the allotted time is unavoidable, ask your guest if it's okay to extend the interview time.

- Don't forget to thank your guest for their time and send them a thank you email afterwards.

Guests provide much more than additional information to your podcast. They make listening much more entertaining and they can potentially bring in readers as well. This is why it is important to get the right guests for your podcast and make sure that they have a good experience on your show. This way, they won't hesitate to come back or recommend other resource people to have as guests on your show.

Chapter 7 – Sharing your Podcast: Where to Post Them and How

Once you've recorded and edited your podcast, you're now ready to share it with the world. The question is – where do you post the audio file and how do you do it? There are many options when it comes to podcast hosting. The choice you make will depend on a number of factors such as your resources, technical know-how, and budget. The method of getting your podcast out there for people to listen to will also vary depending on what hosting option you choose.

This chapter will discuss the different podcast hosting options available and how to upload your podcast using these hosting options.

⬚odcast ⬚osting⬚⬚ here to ⬚pload your Audio ⬚iles and ⬚ow to ⬚o It

You're now on the homestretch. You've got your audio file and all you need is a place to upload it to so that you can share it with the rest of the world. There are numerous options available and each of these options has their pros and cons. Here are some ways you can upload your podcasts and share them to your followers or subscribers:

Take the DIY route

The most straightforward way to get your podcast on the internet is to publish it yourself. This will require having your own server or special software to upload your files to and some technical know-how to be able to create a simple, yet functional user-interface for your website or blog where your listeners and subscribers can access your podcast. If you decide to host the podcast yourself, you have two options for getting it on your website or blog.

- Upload your files to a server.

    o Normally, your website host will act as your server; however, before you do this, you need to make sure that your website's host does not have a limit to the size and number of downloadable audio files that you can upload. Some webhosts are very particular with this because it slows down their servers. If this is the case, check if the webhost offers a premium service that allows unlimited uploads of any size. If so, you can upgrade your service for a higher hosting fee.

    o Once you have uploaded your files, create a download link for it and post it on your blog or website. The link is simply the web address where the file is stored. It will appear on your page as plain text link that the visitors can click on to access the podcast. A right-click on the link will allow the site visitor to download the audio file onto their hard drive. If they do a left-click, however, it may download it or play the file (within the browser or through the computer's default media player) depending on what browser they are using and what plugins they have installed.

    o You can also allow your listeners to stream your podcast through their computer's default media player by creating a text file (.m3u or .pls), pasting the full web address of the audio file into it, and uploading it to your server. After which you can create a download link and post it onto your blog or website.

o If you know enough about writing code to embed the audio file on your blog or website, you can do so in order to have a better user interface. Visitors can click on the in-browser media player to stream the audio file directly from the webpage. The better you are at writing code, the more features you can add like auto-play and more.

o Create an RSS feed so that your listeners can subscribe to your podcast. (More on how to create an RSS feed later).

- Install podcast publishing software

  o There are many free and paid podcast publishing software available for download. Some providers also offer free trial before purchase. Choose one that would suit your needs and match your budget. Some of these software are made for specific operating systems. If you're using Windows, make sure that the software that you've downloaded isn't made for Mac and vice versa.

  o While most podcast publishing software take care of hosting your files as well as distributing them by creating download links, and XML and RSS feeds for you, some still require you to have a server to upload your files to and simply create download links and RSS feeds for the audio file.

Find a Host Online

This is an all-in-one solution for hosting, publishing, and distributing your podcasts. There are so many companies that offer podcast hosting that it can be quite difficult to choose which one is the best. Here are some points to consider when choosing a hosting service for your audio files:

- Bandwidth and storage limits – Free podcast hosting services often have monthly limits when it comes to bandwidth and storage. If you plan to space your podcast releases wide in between uploads, then free services are great; however, if you wish to make your podcasts a weekly affair or if you expect a large amount of listeners to stream your audio, then you may have to pay for premium service that allows for higher or unlimited storage and bandwidth.

- Upload time – This is a minor consideration for people with a lot of free time, but if you want your files uploaded and ready in a hurry, choose a podcast host that offers fast upload.

- Ease of use – Some podcast hosts are easier to navigate and use than others. Look for one that won't confuse you.

- Length of storage – Some podcast hosts may entice you with bandwidth and storage limits that are quite high for a free account. If you encounter a host like this, make sure you read the fine print. It is possible that their free service only allows you to store your files for a couple of months unless you pay and subscribe to their premium services.

- Don't limit yourselves to podcast hosting services. There are some audio sharing websites that people use to upload their own music. These websites can also be useful in storing your audio files. You can embed your uploaded files to your website or direct your listeners to subscribe to your channel on these sites to be able to stream and/or download your podcast.

- Distribution – Creating your own RSS feeds can be tricky if you're not too tech savvy. One way to solve this is to look for podcast hosts that go the extra mile and help you with creating RSS feeds as well.

- Other perks – If you're going to pay extra for premium podcast hosting services, make sure that you get your money's worth. Added features like analytics, podcast statistics, and podcast page themes are nice to have if you're paying for a service like this.

Get it on iTunes

The word "podcast" traces its roots to the iPod, and it's only natural to make your podcast available on iTunes. To do this, however, you would need a server that has a URL that is publicly accessible and that provides support for byte-range requests in order for users to be able to stream your episodes.

For your podcast to be accepted by iTunes, you would need to create an RSS feed and cover art (.jpg or .png). Upload the RSS feed, cover art and audio file to the server and then submit the URL of the RSS podcast feed to iTunes. There are specifications that one needs to follow when creating the cover art and RSS feed. Make sure to follow these specifications before submitting your podcast to iTunes.

⯀reating your ⯀⯀⯀ ⯀eed

The orange RSS icon is one of the most recognizable icons on the internet. Creating an RSS feed is an important part of podcasting. This allows your listeners to subscribe and get updates whenever you come up with a new episode. You are also going to need it if you plan to submit your podcast to iTunes or the different directories you can find online. The RSS feeds generated by podcast hosting services are pretty basic. If you want something that's a little more complex, you will have to create your own.

Creating an RSS feed is really not that complicated. If you know enough about writing code to create your own XML file for your RSS feed, or if you know someone who can do it for you, go ahead and do so. This will allow you to customize the RSS feed just the way you want it. Otherwise, you can download an RSS Creation Software that can do all the dirty work for you. It can be quite limiting, but it makes the process so much easier especially for people who have no idea about how to create an RSS feed.

This type software is usually free to download, but have limited features. There are also paid programs that allow you to do much more with your RSS feeds. You can also opt for free or paid web-based RSS creation services that allow you to manage more than one feed at a time and update your feeds automatically every time you upload a new podcast. If you are looking for an all-in-one solution that will create RSS feeds for your website as well as feeds that follow the specifications set by iTunes, there are special software programs that can do that.

Chapter 8 – Going Live: Take your Podcast to Another Level

While most people pre-record their podcasts, some prefer going live as if they were on-air at a radio station. It isn't as common as recorded podcasts simply because it takes more than just speaking into a microphone and recording one's voice in order to produce a great live podcast. Going live adds a whole new dimension to podcasting. It's spontaneous and interactive – characteristics that recorded podcasts don't have.

Of course, a live broadcast or a webcast isn't technically a podcast because it doesn't meet the characteristics listed previously. It is not downloadable and people cannot subscribe to it using RSS; however, you can still record the webcast and post it on your site as a podcast for subscribers to access, listen to, or download later on.

This chapter will discuss the pros and cons of doing a live podcast, as well as what is needed to broadcast the podcast live over the Internet.

Why Go Live?

Live podcasting isn't for everyone. It takes a lot of guts to speak to an audience even if they can't see you, and like with any live show, a lot of things can go wrong during the broadcast – technical problems could occur, participants may say things that shouldn't be said in public, invited guests may not arrive on time, and so on. With all the things that can go wrong, it begs the question, why go live when you can just avoid all these issues with a pre-recorded podcast?

Despite all of the issues that may come up, people should not be deterred from doing a live podcast because going live can be quite rewarding, especially when everything goes well. Doing a live podcast can do wonders for your website or business. Here are some of the advantages of going live:

- You get immediate feedback. Most of the sites that allow you to broadcast your podcasts live have chat boxes where your audience can type in their questions and their comments. You don't have to assume that they understand the message that you are trying to convey because they'll let you know immediately. This all happens in real time so you can address any questions or concerns they may have regarding the topic you are discussing.

- Live podcasts can be quite fun and entertaining, especially when audience participation is high. It's not hard to be lively and spontaneous when you know that there are people listening to you as you speak. This can add a little (or a lot) more excitement to your program.

- Live podcasts allows you to interact with your audience on a more personal level. Aside from reading comments and questions from the chat box during the podcast, you can also ask listeners to call in and ask you (or your guest) questions and give their opinions on the topic being discussed.

- Going live keeps you on your toes. There's no pausing and no post-production editing to save you from bloopers, dead air, and technical difficulties so if you're up for a challenge then live podcasting is the way to go. Many people consider having all these variables as a disadvantage, but if you are able to handle all these challenges well, you are showing your audience that you are a professional who knows what you're doing and what you're talking about.

- It takes less time to do than pre-recorded podcasts. With live podcasts, you only have to do pre-production work and then proceed to the live broadcast; whereas with pre-recorded podcasts, you need to do some post-production work like editing before uploading the audio file to your website, blog, or to a podcast streaming site.

When should you do a live podcast?

Live podcasts are best done when you already have an audience. Those who already have successful recorded podcasts or popular blogs have a better chance at success with live episodes because they already have a fan base of sorts who are willing to tune in to a live broadcast over the Internet at any given time. If this is the case, there will be no more guesswork regarding whether or not the people tuning in are interested in what you have to say. If you are reaching the right audience, there will definitely be more interaction between you, the podcaster, and your listeners.

You should also consider going live if you are comfortable speaking in front of an audience. Unlike pre-recorded podcasts where you can just pretend that you are talking to yourself, live podcasts elicit immediate feedback from the listeners, so it may seem daunting to someone who is not comfortable with any kind of public speaking.

Live Podcasts vs. Recorded Podcasts

Live podcasts aren't necessarily better than pre-recorded podcasts. The choice whether to record or to go live depends on what type of audience you have and what topics you are talking about.

- If immediate feedback is important to you, then live podcasts are the way to go. Not only do you get feedback from your audience in real time, you can also respond to questions that your audience may have. On the other hand, with pre-recorded podcasts, you would have to keep checking the comment section on your blog or website to find out what your audience thought of your podcast and answer questions one by one on the comment section.

- Pre-recorded podcasts are great when it comes to sharing informative materials like lectures, instructional content, and other materials that can stand alone without any interaction from your audience. With this type of material, doing a live podcast would be useless since you will be doing almost all of the talking and questions and feedback will most likely be ignored.

- One common misconception about live podcasts that needs to be addressed is that in order to broadcast live, you will need a lot of expensive equipment. The truth is that anyone can go live using the same equipment used to pre-record podcasts. The only difference in terms of tools and equipment would be that you need to sign up for an account with a webcasting service (which could be free or for a fee – depending on what services you will be needing) in order to broadcast your podcast live over the internet.

The Disadvantages of Live Podcasts

If there are pros to doing a live podcast, then there most certainly are cons as well. Aside from the chances of experiencing technical problems and creating cringe-worthy bloopers that can't be edited out, there are other disadvantages to going live that one needs to consider:

- You can easily lose track of the topic and time. Interacting with the audience is great, but sometimes, responding to every comment or question posted on the chat box can lead you to go off topic or alienate other audience members who are expecting to hear about something that you have not gotten to because you're too busy responding to questions.

- You may end up spending too much time on a particular topic. This will force you to drop other topics just to stay within your allotted program time. Not being able to deliver on what you promised can lead you to lose listeners – and that's never a good thing.

- Live podcasts are less accessible than pre-recorded podcasts. Not everyone can tune in at the exact time of your podcast. This alienates a big part of your audience. This can be remedied, though, as you can record the live podcast and post it on your website or blog for those who would want to listen to it anytime they choose.

- Live podcasts may be straining on your bandwidth. If you're attempting to do a live podcast from your home computer, make sure you have enough bandwidth to stream the podcast without sacrificing audio quality. One way to circumvent this is to use an external server or an audio streaming server, which can be quite complicated if you don't know what you're doing.

- There are no do-overs during live podcasts. When you make a mistake or if you experience technical difficulties, you can't just stop and start over. You need to be ready for anything that can possibly go wrong while you are broadcasting live over the internet.

⍰etting ⍰p your ⍰i⍰e ⍰odcast

If you already have everything you need for a pre-recorded podcast and are willing to give live podcasting a try, you wouldn't need too much more to do so. Aside from what you already have on hand, you also need to add a few more things to your checklist.

- A subscription to a webcasting platform – It was mentioned earlier in this chapter that broadcasting podcasts live eats up much of your bandwidth and so having an external server or a subscription to an audio streaming or webcasting platform is a must. There are many webcasting services out there. All you need to do is find one that suits your needs the best.

  There are free services available; however, if you're looking for the best services, you may have to be willing to pay for premium services. The cost of monthly subscription varies depending on the features offered in the premium packages.

- Your own /live page – Webcasting and chat platforms usually have an embed code that you can use on your website or blog. Adding a /live page on your blog or website where you can embed your live stream and chat room platform allows you to direct your listeners to just one site, instead of telling them to tune in to your live webcast on one platform and the chat room on another platform. Having your own /live page simplifies things not just for your listeners, but for you as well because you can just monitor everything on one page.

- A chat service – Not all webcasting services offer a chat room for podcasters to communicate and interact directly with listeners. This is especially true for free services as they reserve a lot of their premium features for paid subscription plans. If this is the case, you can utilize a chat service that you can embed on your website or blog so that you can enjoy all the advantages of doing a live podcast.

Once you have all the equipment and subscriptions, you're ready to go live with your podcast. Live podcasts are great when you know what you're doing. If you do decide to go live, make sure that you prepare yourself, put in the work, and have fun with it.

Conclusion

Thank you again for purchasing this book!

I hope this book was able to help you with the basics of podcasting.

The next step is to get ready with your equipment, train your speaking voice, and start recording your first podcast. Simply apply the steps and techniques mentioned in the book so that you will be on your way to becoming successful in this highly popular medium of sharing information.

Finally, if you enjoyed this book, please take the time to share your thoughts and post a review on Amazon. It'd be greatly appreciated!

Thank you and good luck!

Check Out My Other Books

Below you'll find some of my other popular books that are popular on Amazon and Kindle as well. Simply click on the links below to check them out. Alternatively, you can visit my author page on Amazon to see other work done by me.

Android Programming in a Day

Python Programming in a Day

C Programming Success in a Day

C Programming Professional Made Easy

JavaScript Programming Made Easy

PHP Programming Professional Made Easy

C ++ Programming Success in a Day

Windows 8 Tips for Beginners

HTML Professional Programming Made Easy

www.ingramcontent.com/pod-product-compliance
Lightning Source LLC
Chambersburg PA
CBHW071007180526
45168CB00003B/1319